CIVIL WAR TRIVIA

by
Edward F. Williams III

PREMIUM PRESS AMERICA
NASHVILLE, TENNESSEE

GREAT AMERICAN CIVIL WAR by Edward F. Williams III,
Tennessee Historical Commission
Published 1998 by PREMIUM PRESS AMERICA
Copyright © 1998 PREMIUM PRESS AMERICA

ISBN 1-887654-48-8

Library of Congress Catalog Card Number 98-66162

PREMIUM PRESS AMERICA gift books are available at special discounts for premiums, sales promotions, fund-raising, or educational use. For details contact the Publisher at P.O. Box 159015, Nashville, TN 37215, or phone toll free (800) 891-7323 or (615)256-8484.

Cover design and interior design by Bob Bubnis/BookSetters
Cover Painting © 1993 Mort Künstler, Inc., from the original painting by
Mort Künstler, "The High Tide"
Managing editor Carol L. Boker

First Edition 1998
6 7 8 9 10

CIVIL WAR TRIVIA

The events that took place during the 1860s played a significant role in our country's history. Northerners and Southerners, standing up for what they believed, took up the sword against their countrymen—and many times their relatives. Duty and principle led them into battles of desperation, unequaled at any other time in American history, save for the Revolution. More Americans lost their lives in the Civil War than in any other war in American history.

Historians have written, and continue to write, volumes on the Civil War, its battles, and heroes. *Great American Civil War Trivia Book* compiles lesser known facts— tidbits, if you wish—to stimulate the interest of those who know little about the war, as well as those who consider themselves experts on the subject. Read it cover to cover, or peruse it for a few moments at a time. You will delight in facts you've never heard about the Civil War, or The War Between the States, as it's commonly called in the South.

Edward F. Williams III
Chairman,
Tennessee Wars Committee of the
Tennessee Historical Commission
Memphis, Tennessee

1. Robert E. Lee's father, "Light-Horse" Harry Lee, was George Washington's cavalry commander during the American Revolution. He was also the descendant of two signers of the Declaration of Independence: Richard Henry Lee and Francis Lightfoot Lee.

2. Robert E. Lee graduated second in his class at West Point in 1829. He remains the only cadet to complete his degree at the U.S. Military Academy without receiving a single demerit for violations of the college's strict disciplinary code.

3. Future Presidents Abraham Lincoln and Jefferson Davis fought together in the Black Hawk (Indian) War of 1832.

4. West Point's "Class of 1841" produced 20 Civil War generals.

5. Henry Clay was known as the "Great Compromiser" because he opposed civil war and proposed several successful compromises to postpone it. He had seven grandsons; three wore blue and four wore gray during the Civil War.

6. Confederate General George Pickett ranked last in his graduating class at West Point. Union General George B. McClellan was in the same class and ranked second.

7. Jefferson Davis served as the U.S. Secretary of War (1853-57), during which time he introduced the rifle to the U.S. military. This new invention was far more accurate than the standard-issue smooth-bore muskets and, ironically, would give the Union a technological edge in firepower over the Confederacy.

8. Many Civil War generals served gallantly in the Mexican War. George McClellan (USA) and P.G.T. Beauregard (CSA) served on Winfield Scott's staff. James Longstreet (CSA) and Winfield S. Hancock (USA) fought together, as did Albert S. Johnston (CSA) and Joseph Hooker (USA). Robert E. Lee, Joseph E. Johnston, and George G. Meade served as engineers at Vera Cruz, while Colonel Jefferson Davis commanded volunteers from Mississippi at Buena Vista.

9. General Edwin Sumner received the nickname "Bull Head" after a musket ball glanced off his skull during the Mexican War. At the outbreak of the Civil War, Sumner was the oldest corps commander on either side.

10. The youngest enlistee during the war was Edward Black, a 9-year-old musician from Indiana.

11. General Thomas J. "Stonewall" Jackson spent many pre-war years as a professor of artillery tactics at the Virginia Military Institute in Lexington, but he was not an effective teacher. Students nicknamed him "Tom Fool," and one even challenged him to a duel. Professor Jackson would spend countless hours writing his lectures and then memorizing them for class. If a student asked him a question, he would merely mentally rewind his lecture to the section that contained the explanation and then recite his "answer" from that point forward. This practice certainly discouraged follow-ups—and inquisitiveness in general!Robert E. Lee was once Superintendent of the United States Military Academy at West Point (1852-55).

12. Most rifles carried bayonets, but very few soldiers were injured by bayonets.

13. About 80 percent of all wounds received in the war were produced by foot soldiers using single-shot, muzzle loading rifles.

14. James Buchanan served as 15th President of the United States, prior to Lincoln. He did nothing to stop the secession of seven Southern states, proclaiming he could find no constitutional reason to stop them.

15. John Brown was hanged in Charles Town, Virginia, on December 7, 1859. Many soon-to-be-famous people witnessed the event. Among them was Professor Thomas Jackson of the Virginia Military Institute, who attended with a regiment from VMI. The Richmond militia was also present, and in its ranks was a young 20-year-old actor by the name of John Wilkes Booth.

16. As Secretary of War during the Pierce Administration, Jefferson Davis also tried to introduce camels into the military. He believed that these animals would prove useful in the deserts of the Southwest.

17. Abolitionists were the radical forces that desired slavery to be abolished completely. Most abolitionists lived in the North; however, most Northerners were not abolitionists. Racism did exist in the North as well as the South. New York City mobs killed more than 100 blacks during riots there in July 1863.

18. William Lloyd Garrison, a staunch abolitionist, became coeditor of *The Liberator,* a newspaper, first published in 1831, that called for the immediate emancipation of all slaves.

19. Every Southern state except South Carolina had troops fighting for both the North and South.

20. U.S. Grant was staunchly Republican and anti-slavery by 1861. Before the war, however, his actions contradicted his growing convictions. For example, hoping to preserve the Union, Grant actually voted for Democrat James Buchanan in the election of 1856. Moreover, he married into a slave-owning family whose views were pro-Southern. His wife, Julia Dent, brought with her a "dowry" of three slaves. In 1858 he bought a slave by the name of William Jones. After a year, though, he set Jones free and returned his wife's slaves to her family early in the war.

21. Lincoln beat out the favored William H. Seward for the Republican Presidential nomination. Yet Seward, known as "Mr. Republican," would serve Lincoln faithfully as Secretary of State, and would become the target of one of Booth's co-conspirators.

22. Arriving in Massachusetts in 1856, John Brown met the men who would later finance his invasion of the South. They became known as the "Secret Six," and included Franklin Sanborn (a protégé of Ralph Waldo Emerson), Dr. Samuel Gridley Howe (whose wife wrote "The Battle Hymn of the Republic"), George Stearns (who believed Brown to be another George Washington), Gerrit Smith (a former member of Congress), Thomas Parker (a minister), and Thomas Wentworth Higginson (a minister who led a regiment of blacks against the Confederacy). This group helped him raise funds from a wider circle of supporters, including a substantial contribution from wool merchants.

23. Lincoln never met Hannibal Hamlin, his 1860 Vice Presidential running mate, until after Hamlin had been selected by advisors to complete the Republican ticket. Hamlin was from Maine.

24. When John Brown captured the Federal Arsenal at Harpers Ferry, Virginia, the U.S. government dispatched a marine detachment to suppress Brown and his followers. Commanding that unit was Colonel Robert E. Lee of the United States Army. Accompanying Lee was Lieutenant James Ewell Brown Stuart, who would later become famous as Lee's chief of cavalry in the Confederate Army. Both happened to be home on leave from out west.

25. The Federal government did not execute John Brown on charges of treason. Rather, the Commonwealth of Virginia found him guilty of inciting insurrection and sentenced him to death by hanging. However, Brown had participated earlier in several murders for which he was never prosecuted.

26. The U.S. Marines did play a part in the Civil War. In

1859 they helped to overpower John Brown's raid on Harpers Ferry, had a detachment at Bull Run, and had squadrons in the South Atlantic and Gulf blockades.

27. During a 1998 painting job at Harpers Ferry National Historical Park, workers discovered Civil War graffiti dating from Union occupation of the town during 1862.

28. *Harpers Ferry National Historical Park, Box 65, Harpers Ferry, West Virginia 25425; (304) 535-6223. Highlights of the park include the John Brown Museum.*

29. Lincoln and his family resided in Willard's Hotel (14th and E streets) in Washington, D.C., prior to the inauguration.

30. Written by Daniel D. Emmett in 1859 to advertise minstrel shows, the tune "Dixie" became an overnight sensation around the nation. The song later became the unofficial national anthem of the Confederacy. Surprisingly, Emmett was not from the South. He was a native of Ohio and wrote the song in New York City.

31. Robert Anderson commanded Fort Moultrie in Charleston, South Carolina, during the Revolutionary War. His son, also named Robert Anderson, was commander of the fort subsequent to the outbreak of the Civil War.

32. Abraham Lincoln received the 1860 nomination for President at the Republican Convention in Chicago. Oddly, he was not present to accept the honor—an unimaginable occurrence today, but the normal practice then.

33. Many modern-day medical professionals believe that President Abraham Lincoln may have suffered from Marfan syndrome, a hereditary condition resulting in bone elongation and malformations in the cardiovascular system and eyes.

34. In the election of 1860, Abraham Lincoln did not win one Southern district and did not receive any votes in many districts because he was not on the ballot.

35. During the war, the North had many illustrated periodicals, while the South lacked in this area. Therefore, few pictures were made of Confederate social activities during this period. The Southern artists who recorded the war concentrated on military aspects. Luckily, many Southern women kept diaries of the events of the era.

36. The Confederate States of America had a constitution, government, and a capital in less than three months after Lincoln's election. By contrast, the Second Continental Congress took nearly 14 months to declare independence and nearly 2 years to write the Constitution and organize the government.

37. On December 20, 1860, South Carolina became the first state to secede. The legislature's vote was 169 for secession, 0 opposed.

38. In less than two months, the six Deep South states seceded from the Union. Mississippi left on January 9th, Florida on the 10th, Alabama on the 11th, Georgia on the 19th, Louisiana on the 26th, and Texas on February 1st.

39. Alabama played an important role in the creation of the Confederacy in 1861. Montgomery became its first capital. The Confederate soldiers relied on ironworks from Alabama throughout the war and agricultural products early in the war. Although no major fighting took place on land in the state, Fort Morgan (in Gulf Shores), which was a major defense of Mobile Bay until it fell in August 1864, is now a National Historic Landmark.

40. *Fort Morgan, 51 Highway 180 West, Gulf Shores, Alabama 36542; (251) 540-7125. The fort is located 22 miles west of Gulf Shores on State 180.*

41. Tennesseans' attitudes changed on April 14, 1861, when Lincoln called upon state governors to provide 75,000 troops to invade the Deep South. Tennessee's quota was to be two regiments.

42. Nathan Bedford Forrest was among the leaders of the pro-Union forces in Tennessee's first vote on the subject of secession, February 9, 1861. Tennessee legislature approved a military league with the Confederacy on May 7, 1861. However, voters in the state did not approve it until a month later.

43. When the state of Tennessee seceded, Scott County protested and voted to form the Free and Independent State of Scott.

44. Virginia voted to secede from the United States in 1861. However, the state's two pre-war forts—Fort Monroe and Fort Wool (then called Fort Calhoun)—always remained in Union hands.

45. The American flag is known as the "Stars and Stripes," while the first national Confederate flag was known as the "Stars and Bars."

46. Among Confederates, the "Bonnie Blue Flag" was a popular marching song that told the story of the order in which the states seceded from the Union. The song was based on the flag of the same name, which was the first used by secessionists. The flag consisted of a simple rectangular field of dark blue with a single white star in the exact center. Several Southern states briefly adopted this design for their state flag immediately after seceding but before joining the Confederacy.

47. Soon after the first Battle of Manassas, there was a need for a new battle flag due to the similarity of the designs of the Stars and Bars and the Stars and Stripes. A flag for field service was created by P.G.T. Beauregard. Within a year, it became the battle flag for all the Confederate armies and was used throughout the war.

48. Even though there were 13 stars on the Confederate battle flag, there were only 11 Confederate states: Virginia, Tennessee, Arkansas, Texas, Louisiana, Mississippi, Alabama, Georgia, Florida, South Carolina, and North Carolina. The other two stars were for Missouri and Kentucky. Though they technically remained in the Union, they were considered "sister states" by Confederates and furnished many thousands of Southern troops. Both elected Confederate governors and other officials.

49. North Carolina was the last state to successfully join the Confederacy—May 1861. Even though it was a slave state, it did not have the enormous plantations and large black populations of the Deep South. Both Kentucky and Missouri took quasi-official actions to join the Confederacy later.

50. The Upper South included Arkansas, Missouri, Kentucky, Tennessee, Virginia, North Carolina, Maryland, and Delaware. These states provided half the men who fought for the Confederacy, some 425,000 soldiers. These same states sent more than 230,000 Caucasian soldiers and, later, more than 80,000 African-American troops to the Union armies.

51. Maryland was a slave state. When the war began, pro-Southerners in Baltimore attacked Union troops and disrupted rail lines into the city. The possibility of Maryland seceding panicked Lincoln's government into declaring martial law in the state. The official state song still recalls the oppressive Union measures taken during that period of 1861.

52. Clara Barton became proficient at shooting. She could put nine balls within a 6-inch space at a distance of 50 feet, but is remembered as a nurse.

53. Before the Civil War, the South had many military schools, both private and public. These were mostly used to educate young men for civilian life rather than as professional soldiers. Almost all of these closed soon after the war began because their faculties and students joined the Confederate army. However, Virginia Military Institute operated through the war until destroyed by Yankee raiders in 1864.

54. In 1862, the *Chicago Tribune* reported that while many men were slow to respond to the war cause, both Northern and Southern women were eager to volunteer in their places. When they couldn't actually join the fighting, they volunteered as spies, mail riders, guerrillas, scouts, and saboteurs.

55. Volunteer nurses in the Confederacy faced more prejudices against women working around so many men than did their Union counterparts.

56. Well-known as a nurse during the Civil War and founder of the American Red Cross, Clara Barton also is the first American woman ever to run a U.S. government office. President Lincoln asked Barton to search for the Union soldiers missing during the war. She converted her apartment, 11 blocks from the White House, into the "Office of Correspondence with the Friends of Missing Men of the United States Army." In three years, she and her staff identified 22,000 of the approximately 62,000 missing soldiers. The office was only recently rediscovered.

57. Military records indicate that Ella Hobart Gibson was probably the only woman to officially serve as chaplain during the war. She served in that capacity in 1864 for the 1st Wisconsin Artillery.

58. Edmund Ruffin, a Virginia newspaperman, is credited with firing the first shot of the Civil War.

59. Kate W. Howe enlisted in the Union army as Tom Smith, a drummer boy. She was discovered when she was wounded at Lookout Mountain, Tennessee.

60. The women in Troup County, Georgia, southeast of Atlanta, formed a home guard called the "Nancy Harts," in honor of a Georgian heroine of the American Revolution. The Nancy Harts had rifles and muskets and made their own ammunition.

61. The Massachusetts governor sent Harriet Tubman to South Carolina to assist the Union army as a scout and spy. She served as a cook and laundress and was able to guide successful raids and gather valuable information during this time. Even after the war, Tubman never stopped helping people. She opened many black schools in the South, and started a home for the elderly in Auburn, New York, where she died in 1913.

62. Some of the actual female soldiers included Kady Browness and Anne Etheridge, who fought in the Battle of Bull Run. Augusta Foster, from Maine, fought there as well. She had her horse shot from under her, but was able to escape to Alexandria. Mary Galloway fought at Antietam. She enlisted to be near her husband. Mary was wounded, and Clara Barton cared for her during her recovery. The Galloways named their child after Clara.

63. Katie Beattie-Saboteur was well-respected by military leaders for her aid to the Confederate cause. She torched warehouses and Federal boats and successfully helped many prisoners escape.

64. John Watt, President Lincoln's gardener at the White House, confessed to selling official secrets to a newspaper. He was trusted by the President's family because he was a favorite of Mary Todd Lincoln.

65. Belle Boyd's beauty made her an 18-year-old favorite in Fort Royal, Virginia, in early 1862. She used this charm as a spy for the South, helping Stonewall Jackson with military information during his valley campaign that year. She once raced her horse, Fleeta, 54 miles over mountainous terrain to deliver a packet of Federal papers to Jackson. She stole them during a "lover's kill." Captured by Yankees, she was later released and fled to London in 1863, where she went on stage. She died in 1900 during a theatrical tour in Wisconsin.

66. Rose O'Neal Greenhow, a native of Maryland, was listed in the records of the Old Capitol Prison as a "dangerous, skillful spy" for the South. She sent coded messages to General Beauregard. This information helped him plan his defense for the First Battle of Manassas.

67. Future Confederate general Pierre Gustave Toutante Beauregard briefly served as commander of the United States Military Academy at West Point, New York. He took command on January 13, 1861. However, his superiors removed him from his position only four days later, when they discovered that the sympathies of the New Orleans native lay with the Southern cause.

68. Although little is known about many of them, Northerners who believed in the Southern cause often fought for the Confederacy. One Tennessee Infantry company had a mixture of Tennesseans, Irishmen, East Europeans, Germans, and Canadians. Many of the soldiers were from Illinois, Pennsylvania, and Minnesota.

69. At the start of the war, the population of the North was about 22 million people. The South had about 9 million, 3 1/2 million of whom were slaves.

70. Most of the Confederacy's top military leaders came from Upper South states. Robert E. Lee, Stonewall Jackson, Joseph Johnston, Jeb Stuart, and A.P. Hill were from Virginia; A.S. Johnston and John Bell Hood were from Kentucky; and Nathan Bedford Forrest was from Tennessee. However, the political leaders tended to come from the Lower South.

71. Jefferson Davis, of Mississippi, was the favorite candidate among Southern leaders to fill the office of President of the Confederate States of America. He probably would have preferred a commission as a general officer in the army. However, his sense of duty forced him to accept his nomination. His inauguration took place in Montgomery on February 16, 1861. Howell Cobb, of Georgia, was the only other potential candidate considered.

72. Mississippi-born Varina Howell Davis, wife of Jefferson Davis, missed his inauguration to President of the Confederacy. She and their three children joined him in Montgomery on March 4, 1861.

73. The first capital of the Confederacy was originally in Montgomery, Alabama, and was the site of Mississippian Jefferson Davis' Presidential inauguration. It was later moved to Richmond, Virginia, to be closer to the theater of war there.

74. Davis' cabinet members included: Attorney General Judah Benjamin, Secretary of the Navy Stephen Mallory, Vice President Alexander Stephens, Postmaster General John Reagan, Secretary of State Robert Toombs, Secretary of the Treasury Charles Memminger, and Secretary of War Leroy P. Walker.

75. Robert E. Lee rejected command of the Federal Army at the war's outset, because the job would certainly entail an invasion of his beloved state of Virginia. Instead, he accepted the command of the Virginia State Militia.

76. Mary Custis Lee, wife of Robert E. Lee, lived in Arlington, Virginia, most of her life. Lee wrote to his wife repeatedly to leave Arlington, but she had so many valuable possessions there that she was reluctant to do so. Finally, she shipped her valuables to various places, and fled to Ravensworth, her aunt's country home near Alexandria.

77. The small community of Galena, Illinois (pop. 15,000, circa 1860) produced eight Union generals. Among them were John Rawlins, Ely S. Parker (who was also a Seneca Indian chief), and Ulysses S. Grant.

78. U. S. Admiral David G. Farragut practically lived a sailor's life from birth. At 9 years old, he joined the U. S. Navy and fought in both the War of 1812 and the Mexican War. A native Tennessean who married a Virginian, Farragut still chose to fight for the Union instead of following the South.

79. The women of New Orleans took pleasure in offending Federal occupation troops by wearing Confederate insignia on their dresses and holding their noses when Yankees passed by. One Southern belle even emptied a chamber pot on a Federal soldier's head, which led to a decree from General Benjamin Butler. The decree stated that any woman insulting a Union soldier should be held liable and treated like a prostitute. Thus, the general received the nickname "Beast" Butler.

80. The American Civil War is known by some 30 different names. Some of these appellations include the War Between the States, Mr. Lincoln's War, the Second American Revolution, the Great Rebellion, the War for the Union, the Brothers' War, the War to Suppress Yankee Arrogance, the Yankee Invasion, the Lost Cause, and the War of Northern Aggression.

81. The Brothers' War was just that: Brother fought against brother, and families were torn apart over the conflict. Abraham Lincoln had four brothers-in-law who fought for the Confederacy.

82. The opening exchange of the Civil War took place at Fort Sumter in Charleston Harbor, South Carolina. For 38 straight hours, Confederate artillery battered the fort, firing more than 3,000 shells. Not a single man on either side was killed during the bombardment.

83. The Union and Confederate commanders at Fort Sumter, Robert Anderson and P.G.T. Beauregard, respectively, formerly roomed together at West Point.

84. Fort Sumter National Monument is the site of one of the coastal forts built for protection after the war of 1812. It was not completed by the time the Civil War began there in April 1861—and was reduced to rubble by the end of the war.

85. *Fort Sumter National Monument, 1214 Middle Street, Sullivan's Island, South Carolina 29482; (803) 883-3123. Accessible only by boat from City Marina in Charleston or Patriots Point, south of Charleston.*

86. When the war began, the Union Navy could boast only 42 ships on active duty. Under the direction of Secretary of the Navy Gideon Welles, that number would dramatically increase to nearly 700 by war's end.

87. The Confederate Navy was almost nonexistent. Confederate commissioners, however, had ships built in England and then outfitted for war in other countries. In all, 18 vessels were brought into Confederate service in this manner, seeing duty in the Pacific, Atlantic, Arctic, and Indian Oceans.

88. Two of the most famous Confederate raiders were the *Alabama* and the *Florida*. Over the course of their storied careers, they sank or captured a combined total of 102 Union ships.

89. On voyages covering some 60,000 miles at sea, the Confederate ship *Shenandoah* sank 38 Union ships. Her crew captured more than 1,000 Union seamen and did more than 1 million dollars in damage to the Northern cause. She continued to fight three months after Lee surrendered and made her last capture off the coast of Alaska.

90. At the beginning of the war the overall commander of Union forces was General Winfield Scott. An old battle hand, he had commanded the U. S. forces in the Mexican War and had fought in the War of 1812. Extremely overweight and advanced in age, the commanding general of the United States Army could not even mount a horse by himself.

91. In May 1861 the Confederate Congress authorized the enlistment of 400,000 volunteers for three-year terms. The Confederate Army turned away nearly half of the early recruits because they did not have arms and ammunitions to furnish them.

92. Both sides adopted the same trio of colors to indicate the branch of service to which a man belonged. Red trim and striping on the trousers indicated artillery, blue infantry, and yellow cavalry.

93. Southern soldiers had many nicknames, each according to what state he was from.

Virginia	*Tobacco Worms*
Tennessee	*Hog Drivers*
Kentucky	*Corn Crackers*
Texas	*Cow Boys*
Arkansas	*Tooth-picks*
Mississippi	*Sand Lappers*
Louisiana	*Tigers*
Alabama	*Yaller Hammers*
Georgia	*Goober Grabbers*
North Carolina	*Tar Heels*
South Carolina	*Rice Birds*
Florida	*Gophers*
Missouri	*Border Ruffians*

They often called cavalrymen "Buttermilk Rangers" and infantry "Web foot."

94. The Federal troops chose navy blue as the color of their uniforms, while the South adopted gray as their color. However, because of shortages of material, many Southern soldiers dyed their own clothes at home before enlisting. This dye turned their clothes a dull yellow-brown color. Hence, Southern soldiers became known as "Butternuts."

95. Federals called Confederate soldiers "Johnny Reb." Their Northern counterparts received the nickname "Billy Yank."

96. At the first Battle of Bull Run in 1861, the colors of combatants' uniforms were not yet standardized. Some Confederate units wore blue uniforms, while some Northern units wore gray uniforms. Needless to say, the typical confusion of battle exacerbated even further, and several units fired upon their own men.

97. In 1861, Nathan Bedford Forrest enlisted as a private but eventually rose to the rank of lieutenant-general by war's end. He is one of only two men to do this in the course of a single American war.

98. Early on, General Winfield Scott proposed a sure-fire plan to defeat the Confederacy. He called for a naval blockade of all Southern ports and the securing of main waterways, such as the Mississippi, Tennessee, and Cumberland Rivers. The plan was to divide the South into many separate parts and easily overrun them. Scott dubbed it the "Anaconda Plan" because the North would slowly squeeze the will to fight from the South.

99. The first officer killed in the Civil War was Colonel Elmer E. Ellsworth of New York. He was killed on May 24, 1861, in Alexandria, Virginia, after he lowered a Confederate flag from an inn.

100. Virginia had valuable salt mines in the southwestern part of the state. Salt was an essential preservative for meat, and the Rebel army had to have meat to fight. Realizing this, the Union moved toward Saltville in a gambit to cut off the railroad.

101. The Western and Atlantic Railroad, owned by the state of Georgia, transported food and materials from the Deep South to war-ravaged areas of Tennessee and Virginia during the first three years of the war. However, upkeep of the rail system was difficult. Iron rails were hard to acquire. Sometimes rails were taken from one line to use on another that was more valuable to the war.

102. Robert S. Garnett became the first Confederate general killed in action. He was shot at Corrick's Ford, Virginia, on July 13, 1861.

103. The famous Confederate cavalry commander Jeb Stuart wore his U.S. Army uniform to accept his commission from the Confederate Army. In July 1861, as he rode into battle for the first time at Falling Waters, Virginia, he was still wearing it.

104. The Civil War caused a reduction in troops in the West and Midwest. This led to more Indian uprisings, such as the Apache Uprising, Navajo War, and Santee Sioux Uprising.

105. At Manassas Junction, less than thirty miles from Washington, D. C., soldiers fought the first major battle of the Civil War on July 21, 1861.

106. Believe it or not, horse racing flourished during the war years. New tracks opened in Chicago, Boston, and D.C. to join others in St. Louis, Hartford, Louisville, and Philadelphia, to name a few.

107. The Battle of Manassas, or Bull Run, took place near the home of Wilmer McLean. During the fighting, a cannonball crashed through his house, causing great damage to the structure and distress to his wife and children. When McLean relocated his family to a small village called Appomattox Court House, about 20 miles east of Lynchburg, he assumed they had escaped the dangerous sights and sounds of the war's front lines for good. However, in a strange coincidence, the war entered the lives of the McLean family again when they witnessed its conclusion at close range. Generals Lee and Grant used the front parlor of the McLeans' second home to sign the terms of surrender for the Army of Northern Virginia.

108. General Thomas J. Jackson will be forever remembered as "Stonewall." Confederate General Bernard E. Bee bestowed this famous nickname upon Jackson during the first Battle of Bull Run. While his line received a Federal charge, Bee realized that the Confederates were turning the tide of the battle in their favor. Above the clamorous noise of the fighting, he shouted, "There stands Jackson like a stone wall." Moments later Bee was shot, and he died within a few short hours. No one knows if he was criticizing Jackson for not advancing or commending him for standing his ground, but the latter conclusion is most generally accepted.

109. At the outset of the war, most people believed that it would only last a couple of months. However, the first Battle of Bull Run changed the public's view. Few expected Federal troops to be routed from the field by supposedly inferior Confederates.

110. After the Battle of Bull Run in 1861, Confederate troops threatened Washington, D.C. Because of the imminent danger, the Union placed cannons in the hallways of the Treasury and Capitol buildings, and established an army kitchen in the basement.

111. After the first Battle of Bull Run, Confederate troops could have marched on Washington and attacked the capital. However, the unruly Rebels, so elated at their underdog victory, failed to pursue the retreating Federal Army. Joseph Johnston said, ". . . our army was more disorganized by victory than that of the United States by defeat."

112. *Manassas National Battlefield Park, 6511 Sudley Road, Manassas, Virginia 20109; (703) 361-1339. The park is 26 miles southwest of Washington, D.C. off I-66 and Virginia State 234 north.*

113. Civil War battle names varied depending on your affiliation. Federals often named battles after nearby streams or rivers. Confederates named them for nearby towns or communities. For example:

Federal	Confederate
Bull Run	Manassas Junction
Stone's River	Murfreesboro
Antietam Creek	Sharpsburg
Pittsburgh Landing	Shiloh
Tishimingo Creek	Brice's Crossroads

114. The first Confederate military commander in Tennessee was actually a planter from Columbia, Tennessee, and an ordained Episcopalian bishop. General Leonidas Polk served with distinction and honor for the South.

115. Tennessee General Felix K. Zollicoffer became the first general officer to die on Kentucky soil. It was during his first skirmish of the war at Mill Springs, January 19, 1862. His extreme near-sightedness combined with heavy smoke and fog on the field that day resulted in his death. Wearing a white raincoat over his uniform, Zollicoffer mistakenly rode into the lines of an enemy regiment. The Rebels attacked, and the return volley struck him. After killing Zollicoffer, the Union soldiers picked souvenir hairs from his mustache.

116. Simon Bolivar Buckner was Ulysses S. Grant's roommate at West Point and surrendered to him at Fort Donelson in 1862.

117. Fort Donelson National Battlefield, north of Dover, Tennessee, is the site of the first major victory for the North. This defeat forced the Confederates out of Kentucky and most of Tennessee, and gave the Union an edge in trying to gain control of the Mississippi River.

118. *Fort Donelson National Battlefield, P.O. Box 434, Dover, Tennessee 37058; (931) 232-5706. The battlefield is about 80 miles west of Nashville. Visitors to the park can see the Dover Hotel, where General Simon Buckner surrendered to General Grant on February 16, 1862, after both of Buckner's superiors, Generals John B. Floyd and Gideon Pillow, resigned their commands to avoid becoming prisoners.*

119. The Glorietta Campaign of 1862 saw a small Confederate army capture thousands of square miles of Union territory, including Santa Fe. General H. H. Sibley's army was finally driven from New Mexico and Arizona after their supply trains were burned near Pidgeon's Ranch.

120. Nashville, Tennessee, became the first state capital of the Confederacy to fall to Union troops. Union General Don Carlos Buell occupied the city in late February of 1862, less than a year after the outset of the war.

121. Because Confederate raider John Singleton Mosby enjoyed such freedom of movement and popularity in eastern Virginia, that part of the state became known as "Mosby's Confederacy." He and his men were so elusive that he earned the name, "Gray Ghost."

122. Not all of Tennessee was pro-secession. East Tennesseans had few slaves and were strongly pro-Union. In fact, their strong sentiments prompted them to favor secession from the rest of the state. Pro-Unionist guerrillas harassed Confederate supply routes, burned bridges, and terrorized Confederate sympathizers. By early 1862, 25,000 Confederate troops moved in to stabilize the situation. Rebel General Edmund Kirby Smith took one look at the region and said, "East Tennessee is an enemy's country." However, Sullivan and Washington Counties, two of the most eastern counties, were among the state's strongest Confederate supporters, and were long known as "Little Dixie" after the war.

123. The Union ironclad *Monitor* sank in a gale off Cape Hatteras, North Carolina, in late 1862.

124. A Federal sharpshooter killed Confederate General Ben McCulloch, a native of Texas, at the Battle of Pea Ridge, Arkansas, on March 7, 1862. His successor, General James McIntosh, followed him to the grave only 15 minutes after taking command.

125. Arkansas' Pea Ridge National Military Park includes Elkhorn Tavern, which was twice the center of fighting on March 7-8, 1862, as both sides attempted flanking maneuvers.

126. *Pea Ridge National Military Park, P.O. Box 700, Pea Ridge, Arkansas 72751; (479) 451-8122. You can reach the park by driving 10 miles northeast of Rogers, Arkansas, on US 62.*

127. The crew of the Confederate ironclad *Virginia* destroyed their ship at Craney Island during the evacuation of Norfolk, May 11, 1862.

128. The Civil War battle of the Ironclads, between the Union *Monitor* and Confederate *Virginia* (or *Merrimac*), was fought in the Hampton Roads Harbor on March 8-9, 1862. The outcome was a draw.

129. John Ericsson built the *Monitor* with $275, 000 of private capital. The Federal Government agreed to reimburse him *only* if the ironclad were effective against its Confederate counterpart, the *Virginia*.

130. One of the bloodiest battles of the war occurred at Shiloh in southwestern Tennessee. More than 23,000 men were killed, wounded or captured in just two days. Ironically, Shiloh is an ancient Hebrew word that means "place of peace."

131. The Shenandoah Valley was known as the "Breadbasket of the Confederacy."

132. During the Battle of Shiloh, a minie ball struck an artery in Confederate General Albert Sydney Johnston's leg. He soon bled to death. A simple tourniquet could have saved his life, but Johnston's personal surgeon was unavailable because the general had ordered him to help tend Federal wounded elsewhere on the battlefield.

133. After the war, General William T. Sherman was asked which battle was the bloodiest and most horrible of the Civil War. Without hesitation, the battle-hardened veteran replied, "Shiloh!"

134. Reputed to have been a heavy drinker, General Grant was reportedly drunk at both Fort Donelson and Shiloh. Because of his successes, though, President Lincoln supposedly asked an aide to find out what kind of whiskey he drank so that he could buy cases for his other generals.

135. Shiloh National Military Park, at Shiloh, Tennessee, includes more than 3,800 acres, 152 monuments, and more than 475 historical camp and troop positions iron tablets to aid visitors in their understanding of the battle there on April 6-7, 1862. The Shiloh National Cemetery is the resting place of approximately 3,600 Union soldiers, two-thirds who are unknown. (No Confederates were buried there because of the National Cemetery law passed in 1865.)

136. *Shiloh National Military Park, 1055 Pittsburg Landing Rd., Shiloh, Tennessee 38376; (731) 689-5275. The park is located on State 22, 50 miles south of I-40 and 110 miles east of Memphis.*

137. Grant benefited from unusual occurrences. After Fort Donelson, Major General Charles F. Smith was appointed over him. Smith would have been the Union commander at Shiloh except that an infection from a splinter put Smith in bed a week before the battle, and he had Grant reinstated. Smith died of the infection three weeks later.

138. Outside Savannah, Georgia, Fort Pulaski National Monument (now run by the National Park Service) stands in tribute to the 30-hour bombardment of the fort, April 10-11, 1862. Union cannons destroyed the fort, and Colonel Charles Olmstead surrendered before risking explosion of the exposed powder magazines. *Fort Pulaski National Monument, P.O. Box 30757, Savannah, Georgia 31410; (912) 786-5787. The park entrance is 14 miles east of Savannah on US 80.*

139. The first Confederate enlisted man to die was at Fort Morgan, Alabama, in February 1861. The first Union enlisted soldier killed by hostile action was in Baltimore, Maryland, in April 1861. Neither side experienced any deaths during the bombardment of Fort Sumpter, but a member of the garrison was killed in an accident during the surrender ceremony.

140. The Confederate government instituted the first Federal draft on April 16, 1862. It called for all male citizens ages 18 to 35 to be inducted into the army for three years. By February 1864, the range of the age limit expanded from ages 17 to 50.

141. Desertion was common during the Civil War because men felt they had the right to fight near their homes and be with their families during periods of inactivity.

142. Some men who did not fight in the war used the time period for self-advancement while their noble peers were away. Some made their fortunes before the war ended; others set the ground work for long and prosperous careers. Some well-known names on this list included Andrew Carnegie, J. P. Morgan, John D. Rockefeller, Charles Pillsbury, George Pullman, Jay Gould, Marshall Field. Many of these hired substitutes for $300 to take their place in the Army.

143. Lincoln appointed the first general from the Democratic Party, Union General Benjamin F. Butler. During his occupation of New Orleans, which began May 1, 1862, Butler earned the nick-name "Beast Butler," due to his treatment of civilians. He was also known as "Spoons Butler" because he allegedly encouraged the theft of household silverware by his occupation force.

144. After the fall of Norfolk and Portsmouth, the Confederates moved their Navy Yard to Charlotte, North Carolina, a spot more than 200 miles inland! Following the fall of New Orleans, the Confederates operated a Navy Yard in Memphis, more than 500 miles inland.

145. General Jackson received the distinction of being the first to use a railroad for purposes of deception during warfare. He did so at Staunton in May 1862. His "foot cavalry" appeared to head out of the Shenandoah Valley for Richmond, only to covertly return by train back over the Blue Ridge.

146. The most fought over area in the entire nation during the war became the Shenandoah Valley. The town of Winchester, Virginia, for instance, changed hands 76 times.

147. Stonewall Jackson made his career as a soldier in the Shenandoah Valley. Exploiting the landscape, he found ways to use the 40-mile-long ridge "Massanutten" to the advantage of his smaller forces.

148. Although his belief in mystifying the enemy made him reticent to divulge battle plans, even to his subordinates, Jackson prayed so fervently before battle that they could overhear him reciting his objectives aloud.

149. In 1862 Julia Ward Howe wrote a poem without a title. Published in the *Atlantic Monthly*, under an editor's title, "Battle Hymn of the Republic," the verses were later adopted by Union soldiers and sung to the tune of "John Brown's Body." "Battle Hymn" became one of the most patriotic songs of the Civil War.

150. The wounding of Commander Joseph E. Johnston during the 1862 Battle of Seven Pines provided Robert E. Lee the opportunity to take command of the Confederate Army in Virginia. Until that time, he functioned as the equivalent of the army's "chief-of-staff" in Richmond. Appointed by Jefferson Davis on the battlefield, Lee molded his Army of Northern Virginia into one of the most effective fighting forces in the annals of warfare.

151. Very few military maneuvers took place on Christmas Day. This was not because of religious reasons, but mostly because campaigns usually began in the spring and continued until cold weather set in. Severe weather forced the armies to suspend winter activities, so fighting was well over before Christmas. A noticeable exception was the Battle of Stones River in Murfreesboro, Tennessee, on December 30-31, 1862.

152. Music was important in the story of Stones River. Many accounts refer to a battle of the bands on the night of December 30, 1862. Both bands broke into "Home Sweet Home" across the fields that would be strewn with bodies the following day.

153. *Stones River National Battlefield, 3501 Old Nashville Highway, Murfreesboro, Tennessee 37129; (615) 893-9501. The battlefield is situated 27 miles southeast of Nashville.*

154. On Robert E. Lee's first military campaign in 1861, he moved into present-day West Virginia. The excursion was a dismal failure.

155. Before he took active command in the field, General Robert E. Lee received many negative epithets from his troops. They called him "Granny Lee" (because of his aged appearance, although he was only 54 when war broke out) and the "King of Spades" (because he ordered new recruits to dig defenses around the Confederate capital at Richmond).

156. Although the South was rich in raw materials during the war years, it made very few machine tools, steel, rails, munitions, sewing machines, and other war necessities. In Richmond, Tredegar Iron Works remained its most important industrial plant. The second most important military manufacturing center in the latter stages of the war was Selma, Alabama's cannon factories. One of the cannon lathes still sits on the front campus at Auburn University.

157. The chief of artillery for Robert E. Lee's Army of Northern Virginia, William Nelson Pendleton, became a captain in the Rockbridge Artillery at the age of 51. Before that, he was an Episcopalian priest who traded his holy robes for a gray uniform. He named four of his cannons Matthew, Mark, Luke, and John after the Four Gospels.

158. The battle of Sharpsburg (Antietam) almost ended in disaster for Robert E. Lee's Army of Northern Virginia. A careless Confederate officer left his orders outlining the Confederate battle plans in camp. Apparently, he used them as wrapping paper for three cigars. A Federal private found the cigars and orders and sent them on through the chain of command to General McClellan. But McClellan moved too slowly to take full advantage of the information.

159. *Antietam National Battlefield and Cemetery, P.O. Box 158, Sharpsburg, Maryland 21782; (301) 432-5124. Located 10 miles south of Hagerstown on State 65.*

160. During the Civil War, more than 160,000 Irish-born men fought for the Union, most serving in all-Irish units. Brigadier General Thomas Meagher and his "Irish Brigade" fought in legendary battles at "Bloody Lane" (Antietam, Maryland) and Marye's Heights (Fredericksburg, Virginia). However, the best known Irish-born soldier of the Civil War was Confederate Major General Patrick Cleburne.

161. Daniel A. Ridout, a black minister, and his family witnessed parts of the Battle of Crampton's Gap from his home. His parish church served as a hospital after the Battle of Antietam.

162. At the time of the Civil War, other industries besides armaments and farm machinery began. The sewing machine, only a decade or so old during the war, changed the clothing and shoe industries. Men's shirts, which originally took 14 hours to make by hand, were made in a little more than 1 hour. It was discovered that uniforms and shoes made in a few basic sizes would fit most men. This standardization made quantity production simpler and pushed ahead the ready-made clothing industry after the war.

163. Military needs were important to the canned food industry, as well, especially canned milk. Having to produce canned foods quickly and in quantity helped improve machinery in this industry, as well as canning techniques. Vacuum canning had been invented approximately 50 years earlier in response to a contest sponsored by Napoleon to improve food preservation for his armies.

164. Even though some farms and factories were financially doing well during the Civil War, unskilled workers endured starvation, low wages, and sweatshop conditions.

165. During the battle of Antietam, Confederate General James Longstreet and staff operated a single cannon as the crew for a period of about half an hour.

166. General James Longstreet received the nickname "old war-horse" from Robert E. Lee after Longstreet's furious fighting on the Virginia Peninsula in 1862.

167. The term "sideburns" comes from Union General Ambrose Burnside, who sported massive, bushy muttonchop whiskers.

168. A number of colorful Civil War personalities gave rise to a bevy of nicknames on both sides of the fighting:

Gray Fox	Robert E. Lee, CSA
Little Mac	George McClellan, USA
Bulldog Grant	Ulysses S. Grant, USA
Rock of Chickamauga	George Thomas, USA
Stonewall	Thomas Jackson, CSA
Old Peter	James Longstreet, CSA
That Devil Forrest	Nathan Bedford Forrest, CSA
Bull Head	Edwin Sumner, USA
Little Phil	Philip Henry Sheridan, USA

169. Medicines were expensive or hard to come by in the South. Many turned to herbs; however, there was no substitute for quinine, morphine, and chloroform—items that were desperately needed. Smuggling from the North was an important source of supply.

170. In 1862, at Fredericksburg, Virginia, Confederate trenches stretched 7 miles.

171. Virginia's Fredericksburg and Spotsylvania National Military Park is the site of the Richard Kirkland Memorial. Kirkland, a Confederate sergeant fighting at Marye's Heights, crossed a stone wall during battle to give Union troops water and comfort the wounded. The amazed Union soldiers held their fire and gave a cheer. Kirkland died later in battle, but would thereafter be known as the "Angel of Marye's Heights."

172. *Fredericksburg and Spotsylvania National Military Park, 120 Chatham Lane, Fredericksburg, Virginia 22405; (703) 373-4461. The park is located 50 miles south of Washington, D.C. and 55 miles north of Richmond.*

173. President Abraham Lincoln is the only American President ever exposed to enemy fire while in office. On board the tugboat *Lioness* in 1862, Lincoln came under fire by Confederate cavalrymen from shore but was not injured. He also came under fire from Jubal Early's men during their 1864 summer raid on Washington, D.C.'s outer defenses.

174. Jeb Stuart's chief of staff, H. B. McClellan, had a first cousin who was twice commander of the Army of the Potomac, George B. McClellan.

175. Robert E. Lee suffered from heart problems during the war. During the winter of 1862-1863 he suffered a mild heart attack and after the war experienced a stroke that rendered him speechless for many days.

176. The Michigan Cavalry Brigade acquired the finest combat record of any mounted regiment in the Army of the Potomac. They excelled in mounted and dismounted combat throughout the war while incurring more casualties than any other cavalry unit, according to their sometime commander George Armstrong Custer.

177. As a commander, General George B. McClellan's strengths were in matters of drill and organization. Deemed the American Napoleon by the Northern press and nicknamed "Little Mac," McClellan led slow and cautious in battle. Lincoln described him as having "the slows" and once remarked that McClellan had the largest bodyguard in the world—the entire Army of the Potomac.

178. The first three black U.S. regiments were called the Louisiana Native Guard or the Corps d'Afrique.

179. George McClellan introduced innovations into the military, including some in uniforms, tents, and a cavalry saddle that was adopted by the Army in 1856.

180. Jeb Stuart won fame and renown when he embarrassed Union General George McClellan by conducting a raid that completely circled the Army of the Potomac. Absorbing only minimal losses—perhaps as few as one man—Stuart and his 1,200 hussars covered 100 miles in just four days. Boldly dashing around the army's perimeter, they fought only minor skirmishes but captured nearly 200 enemy soldiers, plus about 400 horses and mules.

181. Newspapers occasionally printed colorful editions. When paper was scarce, they resorted to using wallpaper or anything else they could find—just to publish the news.

182. Newspapers were officially censored. No military news could be printed without approval of the general officer in command. This was enforced in most areas in the North and the South. This was probably a result of newspapers from Washington, D.C., revealing so much information early on in the war that they were highly sought by Confederate commanders.

183. During the Battle of Cedar Mountain, August 9, 1862, Stonewall Jackson rallied his men from a retreat and saved the day for the Confederates. He attempted to draw his sword, but because he never used it, the blade had rusted in its scabbard.

184. As the gold supply vanished, the value of Confederate money declined. In 1862, it took $120 to buy $100 in gold. By the end of the war, that $120 rose to $5,500.

185. It wasn't until the fall of 1862 that African-American troops were admitted into the Union army. They were mostly in segregated units commanded by white officers. In the final months of the war, the South considered African-American soldiers, but the public objected and few were ever used in battle.

186. Individual blacks served the Confederacy for extended periods. Louis Napolean Nelson was in the 7th Tennessee Cavalry, CSA, at Chattanooga in 1863 and served the remainder of the war. After the war, he attended more than 30 conventions of the United Confederate Veterans. Louis' grandson, Nelson Winbush of Kissiminee, Florida, is chairman of the national membership committee of the Sons of Confederate Veterans.

187. It took about 19 years for Virginia, Kentucky, and Tennessee to purchase the total 20,000 acres that make up the Cumberland Gap National Historic Park, which was actually authorized in 1940. During the war, the Gap was important to the Confederacy in maintaining its east-west communications and supply lines. The Confederacy lost the Gap in September 1863, which cut off their rail line between Chattanooga and the East.

188. *Cumberland Gap National Historic Park, P.O. Box 1848, Middlesboro, Kentucky 40965; (606) 248-2817. The park can also be reached from Tennessee and Virginia.*

189. The 54th Massachusetts Regiment, led by Colonel Robert Gould Shaw, drew attention as the first African-American regiment raised in the North. This regiment was depicted in the 1990 film *Glory*.

190. Confederate cavalry commander General J. E. B. Stuart raided Fairfax County's Burke Station in December 1862. During the raid, Stuart found time to send a telegram to the Union quartermaster general in Washington, complaining about the poor quality of the Federal mules he had just captured!

191. Considering the combat losses in proportion to the overall sizes of the forces engaged, the Battle of Murfreesboro, Tennessee, saw a higher percentage of casualties than did any other battle. Both sides lost about one-third of their total forces: Confederates suffered over 11,000 casualties and fielded only 34,000 troops, while Federals suffered about 14,000 killed or injured out of 42,000 total. The battle was fought on New Year's Eve, 1862, and spilled over to the next day.

192. The Emancipation Proclamation has been hailed as the greatest executive order ever put into action by an American President. Actually, Lincoln's proclamation was legally useless. It freed slaves *only* in the states in rebellion against the U. S.—precisely where Lincoln had no authority. Slaves in Delaware, Maryland, West Virginia, Kentucky, and Missouri were not freed as a result of the Proclamation.

193. Considered by many historians and doctors to be a classic hypochondriac, Stonewall Jackson constantly worried that his body was out of balance. He customarily raised one arm over his head to allow the blood to flow into the other side of his frame, thus equaling out the amount on both sides. Eating peppers made his left leg weak, and his meals often consisted of bread, milk, and raspberries. He habitually sucked on lemons because he thought it would cure him of his "dyspepsia."

194. Although a devout Christian, Stonewall Jackson gained notoriety for sleeping in church.

195. After being wounded at the Battle of Chancellorsville in May 1863, Stonewall Jackson rested at a nearby residence. At Jackson's request, a servant draped cold towels around his body after the doctors amputated his left arm. The attending doctors knew nothing about the General's self-prescribed treatment. Soon after, Jackson contracted pneumonia and died.

196. The Battle of Brandy Station on June 9, 1863, was the largest cavalry battle ever to take place in the Western Hemisphere. Some 19, 000 men and their mounts fought in this 12-hour engagement. Confederate General J. E. B. Stuart uncharacteristically was caught off guard—surprised from two directions simultaneously—before General "Rooney" Lee arrived to save the day.

197. On June 20, 1863 (two months after Lincoln's official proclamation), Virginia's north-western-most counties seceded back into the Union and formed the new state of West Virginia. It's the only state to have acquired its sovereignty by proclamation of the President of the United States.

198. The epic Battle of Gettysburg started when Confederate soldiers approached the town to get some much-needed shoes. Union troops, on a similar mission, engaged battle with them.

199. The Battle of Gettysburg was the largest land battle ever fought in the Western Hemisphere. In just three days of fighting, more than 50,000 Federal and Confederate soldiers were killed, wounded or captured.

200. Just four days prior to the momentous Battle of Gettysburg, General George G. Meade received the appointment to commander over the Army of the Potomac.

201. At Gettysburg, more than 3,000 horses were killed. The Ninth Massachusetts Artillery Battalion lost 80 of its 88 horses.

202. The 26th North Carolina Infantry went into the Battle of Gettysburg with 800 men. By the end of the battle, only 86 had survived.

203. William D. Pender was the youngest major-general killed in the Civil War. At age 29, Pender, a Confederate, died at the Battle of Gettysburg.

204. John Burns, a native Pennsylvanian and civilian who fought alongside Union troops at the Battle of Gettysburg, gained recognition as one of the heroes of that July engagement. A veteran of both the War of 1812 and the Mexican War, Burns was over 70 years old in 1863.

205. Fifty-one Confederate generals accompanied Robert E. Lee on his failed attempt to win the war on Northern soil at the Battle of Gettysburg. When his army retreated south, however, only 34 generals rode back. Seventeen Confederate generals had died in the bloodiest battle of the war.

206. *Gettysburg National Military Park, 97 Taneytown Road, Gettysburg, Pennsylvania 17325; (717) 334-1124. You can reach Gettysburg by traveling southwest of Harrisburg on US 15.*

207. With no more than 200 men of the 20th Maine Infantry at his command, Joshua Lawrence Chamberlain held a small rocky hill called Little Round Top for several hours at Gettysburg. His men fended off several brigades of Confederate infantry. For his bravery and service to his country, Chamberlain received the Congressional Medal of Honor.

208. Major General Daniel Sickles lost his leg during the Battle of Round Top. He donated his amputated limb to a medical museum and was known to visit it frequently after the war.

209. A massive artillery barrage preceded Pickett's charge at Gettysburg. So deafening was this onslaught that residents in Pittsburgh, 140 miles away, could hear it.

210. At Gettysburg, George Edward Pickett commanded the famous charge that bears his name. During the assault, all 3 brigadier generals and 13 colonels who took part were either killed or badly wounded. Pickett's division lost over two-thirds of its men.

211. Confederate troops from North Carolina advanced farthest in Pickett's Charge at Gettysburg and were some of the last troops to surrender at Appomattox.

212. After the Battle of Gettysburg, the Federal Army's Ordinance Bureau recovered nearly 30,000 rifles and muskets.

213. Gettysburg has been called the "high water mark" of the Confederacy. After Gettysburg, the Army of Northern Virginia never launched a major offensive again and was slowly worn down by superior Union numbers and resources.

214. During the Vicksburg campaign, Grant was injured when his horse slipped on a muddy river bank and fell on him. He was limited in movement for three days. His staff observed that he was fortunate that the horse was not heavier, or he might have had to be replaced as commander.

215. William Henry Harrison Clayton, a soldier in the 19th Iowa Infantry, took part in the siege of Vicksburg and operations against Mobile. However, he's most known for his writings of the war, including battles in the West. In the Battle of Prairie Grove, the 19th Infantry received the highest casualties of any Union regiment on the field.

216. After the siege of Vicksburg, which fell on July 4, 1863, General U. S. Grant held 30,000 Confederate prisoners. Rather than ship them north as prisoners of war on river transports (which he needed for further operations), he paroled the soldiers. He expected them to adhere to pledges that they would not re-enlist and take up arms again for the Confederacy, just as Confederates had been regularly paroling Federal captives during the first two years of the war.

217. In Mississippi, Vicksburg National Military Park, site of the siege that lasted 47 days in the spring and summer of 1863, has a National Cemetery that contains graves of some 17,000 Union soldiers who lost their lives there. Part of the park, the USS *Cairo* Museum displays more than 1,000 maritime artifacts recovered from the Union gunboat that was sunk in the Yazoo River by Confederates.

218. *Vicksburg National Military Park, 3201 Clay Street, Vicksburg, Mississippi 39180; (601) 636-0583. The park is situated at exit 4B east of Vicksburg on I-20.*

219. Lincoln gave his Gettysburg Address at the dedication ceremony of the Gettysburg National Cemetery. However, he was not the main speaker. Edward Everett, a famous orator, spoke for more than 2 hours, while Lincoln's now-famous speech lasted barely 3 minutes.

220. Although he received two devastating and nearly career-ending wounds, General John Bell Hood fought on gallantly for the Confederacy. At Gettysburg, he lost the use of his left arm, and at Chickamauga, doctors amputated his right leg. Subsequently, his aides tied him to his saddle wearing a French-made cork leg.

221. A few Southerners led Union troops into battle. George H. Thomas, a Union leader in the Battle of Chickamauga, was from Virginia.

222. During the 1863 siege of Chattanooga, Confederates blocked off supply routes, trapping Union troops in the city. As the weeks wore on, General Grant issued orders to form a "cracker line," which would feed the troops in Chattanooga. The trail wound its way over the treacherous mountain paths. An estimated 10,000 horses and mules fell to their deaths trying to keep the route open, but eventually enough supplies reached the Union defenders to give some relief.

223. On many occasions, General Forrest, perhaps the most famous cavalry commander of all time, could hardly mount his horse because of severe bouts with boils during 1864, his greatest year of success.

224. Besides 7 miles of self-guided battlefields to explore, visitors to Chickamauga and Chattanooga National Military Park, in Fort Oglethorpe, Georgia, can explore Cravens House, headquarters for Confederate officers and site of severe fighting on November 24, 1863.

225. *Chickamauga and Chattanooga National Military Park, P.O. Box 2128, Fort Oglethorpe, Georgia 30742; (706) 866-9241. Park includes 8,000 acres in southeast Tennessee and northwest Georgia. The park is located along U.S. Highway 27.*

226. General Robert E. Lee realized that Wilmington, North Carolina, was the important link in the Confederacy's supply line from Europe. More blockade runners docked at Wilmington than all of the Confederacy's other seaports combined.

227. Hailed as the "Wizard of the Saddle," Confederate General Nathan Bedford Forrest was a genius as a cavalry commander. However, despite his brilliance on the field, Forrest never received any formal military training and, indeed, had less than two years of any schooling.

228. Wounded in action several times, General Forrest had 29 mounts shot out from under him in battle. One of several commanders to engage in hand-to-hand combat with the enemy, Forrest often entered the fray and fought at close quarters with Federal cavalrymen, killing a total of 30 in different individual encounters.

229. General Lee renamed his horse Traveller because of his untiring endurance over long distances. Although he had other horses during the War, Lucy Long, a mare, was the only other to survive Traveller.

230. A good, reliable horse proved to be invaluable during the war. Some famous ones and their owners include:

King Philip	Nathan Bedford Forrest, CSA
Little Sorrel	Stonewall Jackson, CSA
Dixie	Patrick Cleburne, CSA
Cincinnati	Ulysses S. Grant, USA
Baldy	George Meade, USA
Traveller	Robert E. Lee, CSA
Moscow	Philip Kearny, USA
Virginia	Jeb Stuart, CSA
Rienzi	Philip Sheridan, USA

231. In 1862 after being wounded in battle, Forrest refused an anesthetic as doctors removed the minie ball from his hip.

232. In Alabama, Forrest was in pursuit of Colonel Abel Streight, who, with nearly 2,000 horsemen, was trying to cut off the railroad supply line between Atlanta and Chattanooga. Emma Sansom, a 16-year-old girl, led Forrest to a shallow place to ford a creek, which helped him capture Streight in May 1863, with less than 1,000 Confederates.

233. Forrest, asked about the basis of his military success, said, "I got there first with the most men." Major Charles Anderson, Forrest's adjutant, later altered the quotation to its better known version, "Gits thar fustest with the mostest."

234. The Confederate Army of Tennessee fought in every state east of the Mississippi River with the exceptions of Florida and Virginia.

235. It was well known that Robert E. Lee disliked having his picture taken. Once after the war Lynchburg photographer Pleker asked to take it, the general agreed but suggested that Traveller be part of it. Pleker only took two poses because the flies were so bad that it was difficult to keep the horse still for the time exposures to be effective. Lee did not care for his own photo, but was glad to have so good a one of Traveller.

236. General Robert E. Lee was a brilliant commander who used his undersized, underequipped army to defeat a string of inept Union generals. McClellan, Burnside, Pope, Hooker, and others could never seem to get the best of the "gray fox." For two years and eight months, Lee fended off a series of invasions aimed at Richmond by massive, well-equipped Federal forces, sometimes outnumbering his army two to one.

237. Tennessee's Battle of Franklin saw a larger proportion of the Confederate soldiers killed or wounded than in any other major clash of the Civil War. Only 16,000 Confederate infantry actually took part in the major assault, but of those, 1,750 were killed and 4,450 were wounded. Six generals died in the assault, five were injured, and one was captured. Over 50 regimental commanders were casualties, leaving the Confederate Army of Tennessee with less than 20,000 effective soldiers with which to fight.

238. Unable to pay their property taxes in person—as required by law—General Lee and his wife lost Arlington House (her estate) when the government confiscated it in 1864. Part of the property became the nucleus of Arlington National Cemetery in order to prevent the Lees from recovering the property.

239. Civil War soldiers created their own slang for many terms. The following is a brief sample accompanied by definitions:

bread basket	stomach
greenbacks	money
graybacks	Southern soldiers, lice
pepperbox	pistol
horse sense	smart
top rail #1	first class
hunkey dorey	great
bugger, skunk	officer
snug as a bug	comfortable
sawbones	surgeon
possum	buddy, pal
quick-step	diarrhea
Jonah	bad luck
goobers	peanuts
fresh fish	new recruits
bluebellies	Yankees

240. From 1863 to 1865, Alexandria was the capital of the Restored Government of Virginia, which represented the seven Virginia counties remaining under Union control throughout the Civil War.

241. The Confederacy sent the world's first successful submarine into action in Charleston Harbor on February 17, 1864. However, prior to sinking the *Housatonic,* a blockade ship, the sub *H. L. Hunley* herself sank three times, drowning her crew on each occasion. In fact, Horace Hunley, the vessel's inventor, drowned during one test run.

242. In the fighting that began in early May in the Wilderness and ran through Cold Harbor in early June, Grant lost almost 50,000 men. In one 20-minute stretch at the Battle of Cold Harbor (June 1-3, 1864), 7,000 Union soldiers fell during an assault against fortified rebels.

243. By an odd coincidence, Confederate General James Longstreet was wounded less than 3 miles from the very spot where, one year earlier, Stonewall Jackson had been fatally shot. In both circumstances, the generals were accidentally fired upon by their own men. Unlike Jackson, Longstreet survived his wound and went on to serve Lee until the last days of the war.

244. General Ulysses S. Grant failed to capture Richmond in the spring of 1864. He then attempted to cut off Lee's supply line by laying siege to Petersburg for 9 1/2 months, the longest siege in U.S. history, but not one in which the defenders were fully surrounded.

245. *Petersburg National Battlefield, 1539 Hickory Hill Road, Petersburg, Virginia 23804; (804) 732-3531. Petersburg is 25 miles south of Richmond on I-95.*

246. VMI cadets, some only 16 and others possibly as young as 14, fought in the May 1864, battle of New Market. They charged across a muddy field—later called the "Field of Lost Shoes"—and helped to break the Union lines.

247. Between May 5 and June 30, 1864, the Army of the Potomac suffered more than 61,000 casualties as Grant pushed toward Richmond. Grant's losses exceeded the total strength of Lee's Army at any one time.

248. During a charge that lasted only 7 minutes at the siege of Petersburg, the 1st Maine Heavy Artillery lost 635 men out of 900.

249. Union forces under Nathaniel Banks tried to attack Texas in 1864 by going up the Red River. The campaign ended in a Union disaster.

250. When Washington D. C., came under attack on July 11, 1864, Lincoln went out to view the fighting. He soon came under fire and a young Union captain hastily pulled the President down to safety. "Get down you damn fool, or you'll be shot," the captain said. Lincoln jokingly replied, "Well, Captain, I see you have already learned how to address a civilian." That Union soldier was Captain Oliver Wendell Holmes, Jr., who would later become an associate justice of the U.S. Supreme Court (1902-32).

251. On the infamous "March to the Sea," General Sherman's army, which consisted of 60,000 battle-hardened veterans, destroyed everything in its path that could aid the Confederate war effort. They cut a path of devastation 285 miles long and 60 miles wide.

252. General William T. Sherman and his men received blame for the burning of Atlanta in 1864. However, there is considerable evidence that the uncontrolled fire was accidental.

253. By the time the Savannah Campaign began in November 1864, Sherman probably had the most experienced large Union command. Those who could not stand the strain of a long campaign were weeded out. Many of the men were reenlistments who had fought in many of the major land battles through 1863 or had fought in the Atlanta Campaign of 1864. Because of heavy casualties, the Union Army of the Potomac, although larger, had a higher percentage of new replacements.

254. Union General John Pope caused controversy by holding civilians hostage to prevent partisan raids.

255. Plundering by Sherman's army was widespread, particularly in South Carolina. While many soldiers hoped to accumulate great wealth from the Southerners, others simply destroyed household goods as sheer acts of vandalism.

256. Abraham Lincoln was so certain of his impending defeat at the polls before the 1864 Presidential election that he forced his cabinet members to sign an oath of allegiance to his successor, Democrat George B. McClellan, the disgruntled former commander of the Army of the Potomac.

257. Abraham Lincoln was not only the name of the President of the United States but also of Confederate private Abraham Lincoln from Jefferson County, Virginia. Private Lincoln, who was a member of the First Virginia Cavalry, Company F, deserted in 1864, while the other was re-elected that year.

258. On Abraham Lincoln's first full day in Washington, D.C., he went to Photographer Mathew B. Brady's studio. Brady's assistant, Alexander Gardner, captured five poses of the new President.

259. Lincoln may have received the world's most expensive Christmas gift ever. In December of 1864 the commander-in-chief received a telegram from General William T. Sherman. It read: "I beg to present you, as a Christmas gift, the city of Savannah, [Georgia] with 150 heavy guns and . . . about 25,000 bales of cotton."

260. After horrendous defeats at Nashville and Franklin, General John Bell Hood, commander of the Army of Tennessee, resigned his command in January 1865, on Friday the 13th.

261. General Ulysses S. Grant was the first to hold the rank of lieutenant general (three stars) in the U. S. Army since George Washington, who held the post during the American Revolution.

262. Grant enjoyed a wide strategic vantage point from his position as commander-in-chief of all Union forces for the last 1 1/2 years of the war. Lee held the equivalent post in the Confederate high command for less than three months. He did not receive the appointment to the position until January 28, 1865, far too late for him to be effective.

263. Confederate President Jefferson Davis was imprisoned in Fort Monroe after the Civil War. Today, the fort's Casemate Museum has preserved the cell he occupied.

264. Seven military offensives were directed against Richmond, the primary Union objective all four years of the war. Both McClellan in 1862 and Grant in 1864 came within sight of the State Capitol. "On to Richmond!" became the rallying cry of Union troops. On April 3, 1865, Grant's soldiers finally occupied the capital only a few hours after evacuating rebels had set it ablaze. One-quarter of all Civil War battles and 60 percent of casualties occurred within a 75-mile radius of Richmond.

265. After the collapse of the Confederate government, Union authorities arrested Jefferson Davis and held him in prison at Fort Monroe, Virginia, for two years. He lost his U.S. citizenship and died a man without a country. However, during the administration of President Jimmy Carter (1977-80), the government restored his citizenship.

266. Although he was living in Augusta, Georgia, when the memorable event took place, 8-year-old Woodrow Wilson, future U.S. President from Staunton, Virginia, witnessed the captured Jefferson Davis being transported through town on his way to federal prison. Wilson also recalled seeing Sherman's troops at the front gate of his yard during "the March to the Sea."

267. During the Civil War, Fort Monroe, a Union-held installation, served as a safe haven for hundreds of slaves. It became known as "Freedom's Fortress."

268. At the beginning of the war, only 10,000 families owned more than 50 slaves; three-quarters of all Southern families owned none.

269. By the time General Lee surrendered to U. S. Grant at Appomattox Court House, Virginia, the once invincible Army of Northern Virginia could only field some 27,000 troops.

270. Sailor's Creek was the last significant battle of Lee's final retreat, three days before his surrender. The largest surrender of troops took place there. By the end of the day on April 6, 1865, 7,700 Confederates were taken prisoner.

271. Before a discussion of the surrender terms could get underway between Lee and Grant on April 9, 1865, General Grant, who remembered having met General Lee during the Mexican War, asked his Confederate counterpart if he, too, recalled their meeting. When the latter responded that he did, the two fell into conversation for nearly half an hour before turning to the business at hand.

272. When Lee surrendered to Grant at the McLean House, many Union officers were present to witness history taking place before them. When it was all over, General Philip H. Sheridan offered to buy the table used to sign the terms, but McLean would not agree to sell. Sheridan gave McLean cash and took the table anyway. Other Union officers—not offering a single penny to McLean—made off with chairs and tables used by the principals and stripped the historic room of all its furniture.

273. The terms of surrender to which Lee agreed at Appomattox Court House stipulated that all Confederate soldiers who owned their own horses could keep them. Also, all Confederate officers could keep their sidearms and swords. Both minor concessions were gestures of magnanimity from Grant.

274. April 9, 1865, the date of General Robert E. Lee's surrender to General Ulysses S. Grant, fell on Palm Sunday.

275. *Appomattox Court House National Historical Park, State Route 24, Appomattox, Virginia 24522; (804) 352-8987. Appomattox is about 90 miles west of Richmond.*

276. Although the war was officially over on April 26, 1865, when Lieutenant General Joseph E. Johnston surrendered the Army of Tennessee, the last land skirmish took place on May 13, as Edmund Kirby Smith and his troops battled with Federals at Palmito Ranch, near Brownsville, Texas. This skirmish saw the Union troops retreating, which, ironically, was a Confederate victory. Smith surrendered on May 26. The confederate warship, *Shenandoah,* surrendered to British authorities November 6, 1865, at Liverpool.

277. The American Civil War began on April 12, 1861, at Fort Sumter, South Carolina. It ended on April 9, 1865, at Appomattox Court House, Virginia, almost exactly four years to the day it started.

278. On April 14, 1861, Major Robert Anderson lowered the United States flag flying over Fort Sumter. Exactly four years to the day later, April 14, 1865—the day Lincoln was shot—the same Major Anderson raised the flag again over Fort Sumter. Lincoln died on the morning of April 15.

279. The President and Mrs. Lincoln went to Ford's Theatre on April 14 to see *Our American Cousin.*

280. *Ford's Theatre, 511 10th St. N.W. Washington D.C. 20004; 1 (800) 889-2367*

281. When he leapt onto the stage of Ford's Theatre after fatally shooting President Lincoln, John Wilkes Booth reportedly shouted, "Sic Semper Tyrannis" ("Thus Always to Tyrants"), Virginia's state motto. Before the war, Booth was a member of the Virginia Militia and was present at the execution of John Brown.

282. John Wilkes Booth's first plan was merely to kidnap President Lincoln and members of his Cabinet. However, when he realized that he could not possibly get near the President, he decided to assassinate him instead.

283. Edwin Booth, brother of John Wilkes Booth, once saved the life of President Lincoln's son Robert.

284. More men died from disease and sickness than from battlefield deaths during the Civil War. For each soldier who died in battle, two died from illness.

285. After being shot in the back of the head at Ford's Theater, President Abraham Lincoln was moved across the street to the home of William Petersen, a tailor. Ironically, John Wilkes Booth, as a lodger, once occupied the room and bed where Lincoln died.

286. Andrew Johnson, a native of Tennessee, became his home state's wartime governor when he received the appointment by President Lincoln in 1862. Johnson, a Democrat, would run as Vice President with the incumbent Lincoln, a Republican, on the Union Party ticket in the 1864 Presidential campaign. Upon Lincoln's assassination, he would become the nation's 17th President.

287. Covering 40 acres with a capacity to handle 3,000 wounded soldiers, Richmond's wartime Chimborazo (Hill) Hospital was the largest hospital ever built in the western hemisphere up to that time.

288. Jefferson Davis was held in prison for more than two years but never stood trial. Besides charges of treason, he also was accused of having conspired in the assassination of Lincoln. That accusation was never proven, but Davis never got to defend himself.

289. CSA President Jefferson Davis never discovered that there was a spy in Richmond's Confederate White House—until it was too late. Mary Elizabeth Bowser, the Davis family's freed black domestic employee, used her position in the President's household to access top-secret information, which she then relayed to undercover Union operatives within the city. Called "one of the highest placed and most productive espionage agents of the Civil War," she has been enshrined in the U.S. Army Military Intelligence Corps Hall of Fame.

290 Called the first "modern war," the American Civil War introduced many "firsts." These include the U. S. Secret Service, the Medal of Honor, the income tax, a viable machine gun, naval torpedoes, repeating rifles, battlefield photography, and the first African-American U. S. Army officer (Major M. R. Delany).

291. The U. S. Civil War saw nearly 6,000 skirmishes and battles. In addition to the more familiar Civil War landscapes of Pennsylvania and the Southeast (Virginia, Tennessee, Georgia), other hostilities between Federals and Confederates also took place. Oregon, Ohio, Indiana, California, New Mexico, Arizona, Utah, Idaho, Vermont, New York, Illinois, and the Russian territory, which would later become Alaska, were some of the sites.

292. California was far from the battlefields; however, conspiracies took place among Southern sympathizers and rumors of invasion persisted. Fort Mason, on the San Francisco bay, was part of the defenses. Strong sympathy for the Confederacy resulted in virtual occupation of southern California by Union troops raised in California.

293. General John Hunt Morgan, known as the "Rebel Raider," was once believed to lead the only Confederate invasion of Ohio; however, Brigadier General Albert Gallatin Jenkins and his troops moved onto Ohio soil a year earlier in 1862. Both raids took place around Buffington Island.

294. When the war commenced, the United States had 15,259 enlisted men and 1,108 officers on active duty. By war's end, nearly 3 million men served in the military.

295. Morgan's Raiders made up two seasoned brigades: Kentucky regiments, led by Colonel Adam "Stovepipe" Johnson, and some Kentucky and Tennessee cavalry regiments, led by Colonel Basil Duke, Morgan's brother-in-law.

296. The Gracie Mansion, traditional home of the Mayor of New York City, was originally the home of Confederate General Archibald Gracie.

297. By the time of the surrender of Robert E. Lee, the U. S. government had bought and paid for approximately 840,000 horses and 430,000 mules.

298. Many Civil War-era firearms were notoriously inaccurate. One expert estimated that for every Confederate soldier shot in battle, the Union needed 240 pounds of gunpowder and 900 pounds of lead to achieve the result.

299. Captain Sally Tompkins, born at Poplar Grove, Virginia, was the only woman granted a commission in the Confederate Army. She founded and directed Robertson Hospital in Richmond between 1861 and 1865.

300. The death toll for the Civil War rose to almost 700,000. This number exceeds the death tolls from all of America's other wars—from the Revolution to the Persian Gulf—combined.

301. Prisoners-of-war suffered many hardships in both the North and South. Exposure to inclement weather, disease, hunger, tainted drinking water, and foul sanitary conditions took a horrible death toll. Of nearly 200,000 prisoners held in the South, about 30,000 died. The North incarcerated nearly 230,000 POWs, and about the same number died.

302. Native Americans and African-Americans contributed greatly to the Union war effort. Of the 3,530 Native Americans who fought, 1,018 were killed, or almost one-third. Some 180,000 African-Americans fought for the North and more than 36,000 gave their lives. One Native American to become a general was Confederate Brigadier General Stand Watie. An unknown number of African-Americans served the Confederate Army, including 45 with General Forrest. Of those, 44 survived the war, and 38 went with him to his farming operation in Mississippi after the war.

303. Salisbury Prison in North Carolina served as the Confederacy's second-largest Civil War prison.

304. Shortly after falling ill in 1870, Robert E. Lee died in his parlor at home in Lexington, Virginia. His last words were reportedly, "Strike the tent."

305. The only man arrested and convicted of war crimes during the Civil War was actually born in Switzerland. Henry Wirz served as commandant of the notorious Andersonville Prison in Georgia. After the war, the government arrested, tried, convicted, and hanged him for starving the disease-ridden Union prisoners under his command. The percentage of deaths at Andersonville was only slightly higher than that at the Union prison camp at Elmira, New York.

306. One of the highest honors a soldier could achieve was to carry the flag in battle. However, flag-bearers were prime targets for enemy fire, and their chances of being shot were considerably higher than those of the average soldier.

307. General officers suffered the highest casualties of the war. A general's chances of being shot and killed in battle were 50% higher than those of a private.

308. Overall, the Confederate States of America commissioned 425 general officers during the Civil War. Of that number, 77 (18%) were killed or died of wounds received in combat.

309. The youngest general officer of the war was Brevet Major-General Galusha Pennypacker of the Union. Born on June 1, 1844, Pennypacker was only 17 at the outset of the war. He remained too young to vote until the war's end.

310. At the conclusion of the war, former Tennessee Governor Isham G. Harris fled to Mexico because of a $5,000 bounty placed on his head. Former U.S. Vice President and Confederate General John C. Breckinridge fled to Cuba and then England.

311. After the war many generals, North and South alike, found it difficult to adjust to civilian life, but others achieved extraordinary success. Robert E. Lee became president of Washington College in Lexington, Virginia (which today bears his name as well), while Ulysses S. Grant became the 18th President of the United States. In 1869, William T. Sherman became the highest-ranking general in the U. S. Army. James Longstreet held many federal posts, such as surveyor of customs in New Orleans, minister to Turkey, and U. S. marshal for Georgia. And residents of Maine elected Joshua L. Chamberlain governor four consecutive times.

312. Six Union officers ascended to the White House and the nation's highest office: Ulysses S. Grant, Chester A. Arthur, James A. Garfield, Benjamin Harrison, Rutherford B. Hayes, and William McKinley.

313. General Robert E. Lee died in October 1870, never knowing whether Congress ever received or acted on his appeal requesting a pardon and restoration of his citizenship. By chance, in 1970 a scrap of parchment turned up in an old desk in the Library of Congress. The document proved to be Lee's original letter to then-President Ulysses S. Grant, pleading for the restoration of his rights as an American citizen. So after more than a century, Congress finally addressed the matter, and restored Robert E. Lee's citizenship. Yet even after such a long period of time, bitter feelings still remained; the vote was *not* unanimous.

314. Both Stonewall Jackson and Robert E. Lee called out Confederate General A. P. Hill's name on their deathbeds. Jackson reportedly said, "Tell A. P. Hill to prepare for action." Lee supposedly uttered, "Tell Hill he must come up!"

315. The Civil War saw the first conscription acts, implemented by both sides. However, a wealthy man could "buy" a substitute to fight in his place. Poor men could profit by selling themselves as substitutes—if they survived. This loophole gave rise to the phrase, "A rich man's war but a poor man's fight." The Confederate Congress abolished the practice in 1863, but the Union continued to allow payment of $300 for a substitute.

316. Besides George Washington, Robert E. Lee has more articles and books written about him than any other American.

317. Confederate Major General Joe Wheeler returned to the U.S. Army in 1898 with the rank of Major General, thus becoming one of only two men to hold this high rank in both the armies of the CSA and USA.

318. Former Confederate General Joseph E. Johnston was considered one of the South's "shining stars" in the Civil War. In 1891, 26 years after the war, he died of pneumonia, a sickness that was then almost always fatal. Oddly enough, he contracted the illness after serving as a pallbearer at a funeral service for his wartime nemesis and postwar friend General William T. Sherman. Prior to that somber occasion, he also served as a pallbearer at the funeral of President U.S. Grant.

319. Simon Bolivar Buckner, the last surviving Confederate general, died in 1914.

320. Walter Williams, the last reported surviving Civil War veteran, died on December 19, 1959, at the age of 117. Once a forager for Confederate General John Bell Hood, Williams survived the last of the Union veterans by three years.

321. The McLean House, which currently stands in Appomattox Court House, Virginia, is not the original home where Lee surrendered to Grant. Disassembled in 1893 for an exhibition in Washington, D.C., the original was never reassembled. In 1948 the Federal Government built a copy on the site of the original, and in 1950 the National Park Service dedicated the replica. Robert E. Lee IV and Ulysses S. Grant III, descendants of the men who made it famous, served as honored guests at the ceremonies.

322. *Wilson's Creek National Battlefield, Route 2, Box 75, Republic, Missouri, 65738; (417) 732-2662. Republic is about 10 miles southwest of Springfield.*

323. For most of the Civil War, Lee was not the highest ranking Confederate officer. That distinction went to Samual Cooper, the Confederacy's Adjutant General.

324. Mowers and reapers were still fairly new machines when the war began. These devices saved human labor and could be used by women and children. During the war, Northern farmers produced large quantities of corn, oats, and wheat to fill domestic needs, and also sold large amounts to England. The antecedents of the International Harvester Company enjoyed great growth during the war years.

325. Kendrick Place, a half-mile north of Carthage, Missouri, served as a haven for both Union and Confederate armies. General Joseph Shelby and 600 Confederate soldiers camped on the grounds, as did General Sterling Price and his men. Major General Franz Sigel, commander of Union forces, also set up headquarters there on some occasion. Shelby has a unique distinction. He never surrendered after the war, although he returned to Missouri and held elected office.

326. Very few monuments are found at Wilson's Creek National Battlefield in Missouri. One, however, is dedicated to Union Brigadier General Nathaniel Lyon, who lost his life in the charge up Bloody Creek. Self-guided tours take visitors around the almost 5-mile route of the battlefield.

327. *Nathan Bedford Forrest State Park, is located about 7 miles northeast of Camden, Tennessee at 1825 Pilot Knob Road, Eva, Tennessee 38333; (901) 584-6356.*

328. *Parker's Crossroads National Battlefield, Located on I-40, exit 108, halfway between Memphis and Nashville, Parker's Crossroads, Tennessee 38388. (901) 967-3508.*

Mort Künstler

"Whatever labels are assigned to Mort Künstler and his art, it is certain that his paintings will continue to be recognized for their strong and effective compositions, for the accuracy of their historical documentation and for the dramatic way they record the American Spirit."

—M. Stephen Doherty
Editor-in-Chief
American Artist Magazine

Considered America's reigning dean of historical artists, Mort Künstler's work is well known throughout the land.

A commission from CBS-TV in 1982, to do a painting for the mini-series, *The Blue and the Gray* directed his interests toward the Civil War. Since then, his work has been published in several books including *The American Spirit—The Paintings of Mort Künstler,* (published in 1994 by Rutledge Hill Press), *Images of the Civil War, The Paintings of Mort Künstler* with text by Pulitzer Prize winning author James McPherson, (published in 1992 by Gramercy, a division of Random House). A one hour A&E special by the same name aired on April 30, 1993 becoming the first television show featuring one artists work on the Civil War.

His reputation for both accuracy and artistic mastery earned Künstler a commission from the U.S. Postal Service to do a painting of the Buffalo Soldiers. The stamp was issued in April of 1994.

Künstler's painting, *The High Water Mark*, was unveiled at the Gettysburg National Military Park Museum during the 125th anniversary observation of the battle, and is considered by experts to be the most accurate and exciting painting ever done of the event.

Probably no other artist has recorded so many events in the history of America, and certainly no one has done them with such extraordinary authenticity and drama as Mort Künstler.

To get a catalog of high-quality limited edition prints of the artwork of Mort Künstler please contact:

American Print Gallery
P.O. Box 4477
Gettysburg, PA 17325
Phone 800-448-1863
Fax 800-942-1861
www.mkunstler.com

Premium gift books from PREMIUM PRESS AMERICA include:

I'LL BE DOGGONE

CATS OUT OF THE BAG

GREAT AMERICAN CIVIL WAR

GREAT AMERICAN GOLF

GREAT AMERICAN OUTDOORS

GREAT AMERICAN GUIDE TO FINE
  WINES

GREAT AMERICAN WOMEN

ANGELS EVERYWHERE

MIRACLES

SNOW ANGELS

THE POWER OF PRAYER

GOLDEN TRUTHS, OT

ABSOLUTELY ALABAMA

AMAZING ARKANSAS

FABULOUS FLORIDA

GORGEOUS GEORGIA

SENSATIONAL SOUTH CAROLINA

TERRIFIC TENNESSEE

TREMENDOUS TEXAS

VINTAGE VIRGINIA

TITANIC TRIVIA

BILL DANCE'S FISHING TIPS

AMERICA THE BEAUTIFUL

DREAM CATCHERS

STORY KEEPERS

THE STORY OF GATLINBURG

Great Reading.   Premium Gifts.